Fire, Ice and the Heart

A Collection of Poems
by
Margarita Zubkus

For my dearest Alexis

At the touch of love everyone becomes a poet.

– Plato

CHAPTER ONE

New York City
1997

Love can sometimes be magic. But magic can sometimes...
just be an illusion.

- Javan

Let Go

Let Go

      It's too hard,

      Too easy.

It's as silly

      as the morning milk spilt on the floor,

      as a child's laugh in the zoo,

      as the day.

I smile at the stupidity,

laugh at the irony.

Just turn around. We are not Orpheus.

Stubborn, resentful –

      blindly we forgive but never go back.

A Message

A Smile — a message?
No! A smile.
A tear — a fear?
No! A tear.
A touch — a grasp?
No! A touch.
Love — a weakness?
No! Life.

A Space

My eyes are wet, lips dry.

The pain in my heart... no, it cannot be the heart.

       Liver? Kidneys?

Not a pain, a space.

Yes, a space, a hole.

No, I am full, very full.

Full with... yes, a space.

It's good. It's good.

Reliability of Change

Gusts, the gulls carry,
giving way to Her whims.

Serenity, eternity bring the brooding waves
breaking on the beach.

Sandy shells swept on the shore
by the waves, brought back to the ocean
and cleansed once more.

As the gulls fight, the waves roar.
I ask why, forever it was, never more to be.

Look

Look Mama. I am free. I am all alone!
Look at me. I am a man. Aren't you proud?
I am alone.
I have no one to love and no one loves me.
I am free.
I can say "me" and not "us".
I can say "I" and not "we".   Don't you agree?
Isn't that free?

I'll have no children to worry about.
You'll have no grandchildren to see.
I am free. I am free!
I am free to be alone.
I will be old alone; you will die.
But I will be free.
You will have no daughter to hold.
You will be free.

Look Mama. I am alone.
I am alone.

We Forget

Time, ticking – endless.
We forget. How fickle we are!
How fragile we are.

To Feel

Today there is no wind.

No storm, no breeze.

The water is placid.

No ripples, no waves.

The heat becomes stifling.

The sailboats are still.

The loneliness impenetrable.

We go about our days.

A word or two,

a smile or thought.

Oh, the air is so thick!

The pleasantries so bland!

If only a breeze. If only a breeze.

A Fire Inside

Inside you a fire rages.
　　　The flames singe my hair.
　　　The smoke blinds my eyes.
Tears fall. The drops fill an ocean,
　　　though the fire is not quenched.
A fire so cold, it freezes your love.
　　　So strong, it makes me weak.

Go Away

Oh cruel Destiny ! The mockery is shameful.

     Your face so innocent; the pain so flagrant;

     the temptations so putrid!

Oh blasted Fate! I can feel your body.

     Your hands caress, while your fingers suffocate.

     You dance in the light, but your shadows us blind!

Oh blessed Karma! What kind of creature are you?

     To see joy in my crippled stride,

     grotesque satisfaction in the endless suffering I endure.

Go All! Be on your way. Leave me alone.

Take your music and take your spoils.

Just go. You are done here.

With me you are done.

A Cruel Joke

Dear Mr. Freedom, what a lie you spread.

What a game of deceit. Your temptation you

slap across my face!

"Be free", you shout at me mockingly as

all applaud your pomposity.

Oh, Mr. Freedom, how naïve your childish play is.

For, to lie alone naked in my bed, I am not free.

I am no longer free to love the man who used to lay beside me.

So Mr. Freedom, your song of praise will not spring from my lips.

Be not so proud, for in you I am locked in a prison of emptiness.

My Heart

Old Raven, I set out my heart for you.
 Would you prefer a plate?
It's not yet too bitter, though a bit cold.
Please, do not turn away.
Come eat, old Raven, it no longer beats.
 It nourishes me no more.
The vultures do not want it, for it's not yet dead.
 It just fits me no longer.
Old Raven, come. It's not a bad heart.
 It just loves the wrong one.

For Warmth

I lie naked in my bed.

The window is open.

The wind rushes in.

My eyes slowly close.

The sheets lightly cover my bare skin.

Alone I am.

Yet my body sighs

as I feel you lay your arm across my back.

My heart swells as you glide your soft lips

gently across my breasts.

My spine quivers as I feel you rest

your warm breath upon my nape.

I awake.

I pull my precious sheets around my fainted flesh.

Wrap them tightly around my body, coiled as a frightened snake,

for warmth no longer found.

So Distantly Near

The journey you make, my Love.

brings oceans between us.

The wars you battle

leave my heart lonely and troubled.

The prison that chains you

locks out my unyielding love.

So far far away you are coldly swept from me.

The pain of being apart is a weight my soul

can no longer bear.

Oh this loneliness we both bear!

The love we nurture inside.

Oh, the pain of it all as I watch you cross the street.

Too Busy

I have no time – too busy – I cannot.

Of course, I am sorry.

A movie, maybe? A show? Something light?

Oh no, you understand, just too busy.

A coffee, here, in the park, by the tree?

I have no time, the clock is running.

Then a hug, a simple touch, maybe a kiss?

I cannot. I have no time. I am so tired.

Come, then after work, lay in my arms – sleep.

No, I mustn't. To sleep in your arms I have no time.

A thought? A care? A whisp of love?

No, I am sorry. To love you I cannot.

I will not find time.

I do not have the love.

I Can Feel

I can feel the heat of your body
as I pull the blanket into my naked breasts.
The night is dark, but I can see your image
on the pillow that lies fallow next to mine.
It's all an illusion, a confusion that devours
the most precious piece of my tormented heart —
the part I gave you —
the part you threw back,

       untouched, unwanted, unloved.
Shattered, I try to gather the pieces.
Rejected, bleeding and sore.
A beating puzzle that cannot be solved.

An Opening

Mountains of memories,

beautifully clear, marvelously muddled.

Forests of future hopes,

frozen in time, melting from the fires.

Oh the fires! Fierce and frantic – forgetful.

Forgetful of the love that warmed and not burned.

Plain and placid in the painful present,

unable to go back - the joyous past

infected with too many poisons.

Stagnant and stale, no place to go.

A future soiled, stolen from my womb.

The freedom to be and see "me",

here and today – it lightens, refreshes, clarifies.

CHAPTER TWO

Moscow
2001 – 2002

There is love of course. And then there's life, its enemy.

- Jean Anouilh

Trapped

The darkness weighs heavy on my spirit.
A flower to grow sprouts but sits dormant.
No energy to shiver, shout or cry,
trapped from song and dance,
alone and scared, fooled and used.
Naïve or kind? Ignorant or hopeful?
Appoint me queen, elect me jester.
An organized mad house in any case.
A new form of poetry emerges and rots,
rancid and putrid, contemplative and heroic.
Or driven by egoism and fear.
All is circular, nothing novel.
But fret, fret, fret we all — futility.
Slink like a panther and maintain your beauty
for all is appearance and attitude.
Aptitude for non — wings in the wind.
Struggle to stay a flight. To go.
To where? To fall again.

Lost Communication

Faculties, faculties – keep your faculties.
Never were they nurtured, fed or formed.
Level buildings or level the unbalanced.
Look at the field of lost communication.
Call forth the armies and the gods
and never forget Your alphabet.
Sit, stay, beg and chew your own bones.
Battered and flowered, fried and baked,
like a madman your head goes porous.
So let the pollution flow through and out.
Spit and turn with fires below.
Clouds engross and squeeze
red silk from a worm in the tequila.
Wrap yourself like a present in scarlet.
Stay warm and give yourself up.

Cashmere Rain

It's often blue - cashmere rain. Like an antidote,

freeing the trapped from self strangulation,

those suffocating from their own greed.

Velour is nice, but fake and cheap.

What's real counts. Yes! For whom?

Not me. Be naked then, and freeze.

Or burn. Is there another way?

Is there a way? Out? In? Okay, around.

Around, always around and around – that's easy.

Roar and rant, rave and repeat.

Be like the ocean and regurgitate,

for nothing is new – don't even try.

Repeat, repeat, re- peat, rep –eat, reap – it.

Disregard the others; ignore the rest.

You win, you loser.

Chaos

I fail to grasp the meaning of life.

It's a masterful plan created by God.

A silly chess game – no plan at all.

Simple chaos made fun of.

A dead puppet, rickety and stupid,

passing through each day, each night, each day…

Forget, remember. Who cares.

A merry-go-round with horses bobbing

up and down and up and down.

The music plays, the cotton candy sticks to your teeth.

Your mouth is pink. Your stomach is sick.

Get off the ride, but leave your head spinning.

Or is it the world spinning around you?

It's wearing thin, this cubicle. Tired of it!

Rise above it! You are better than this!

Ha! Do not pass Go; do not collect a hundred dollars.

Go straight to jail.

But you just got out!

You were never out.

I am a Candle

What if you were a candle?
Lit up, blown out, melting.
Burning, giving off warmth.
Emitting smoke, shedding your layers.
Left deformed, left without your spine.
Shrunken to form a pancake of useless wax.
Blackened by fires.
Peeled off your post by a knife with no mercy,
chipping your pieces and breaking your core.
But how pretty you were in the store.

The Vulnerable Soldier

Oh the gallantry! The pageantry that makes
it all worthwhile.
To keep one's faith; to distract and deny.
Forthwith the flurry of fastidious fancy!
The pompous insanity that is so infectious.
Leave destitute the insipid philosopher,
deprive her of her distasteful attempt
to deny the Emperor his clothes.
Carry on, young warriors, your wasted battles,
for the Fatherland feeds on your ignorance.
Stand soldiers of misfortune for the mystery
that is theirs, and never lose sight of the sacred – the God,
The god that is ours and only theirs if it is ours.
Sprint, sputter, spring and sling, but do not
Stop. Do not stand, for they will make you fall.
Awareness is sin, be bold but dumb.
Carry a shield, but have no guard, for
vulnerable we must remain.

Your Eyes

Lift your eyes; I see only your lids.
Are you afraid of what you'll see?
Your frigid breath, your stone cold stare.
Lips quiver like droplets in the wind.
This I can no longer bear. A lock of hair
drops across your face. You swallow,
breathe, sigh – a sign of life.
Have you left? Are you leaving?
I witness your tracks in the snow.
I sink in your vulturous void.
Foul! Pull down your lids and
cover the black hollows that
leave you blind.
Let darkness be your guide.

The Apologists

An apiary full of apologists!
A blasphemous cauldron of hypocrisy!
Ah, this anesthetized panacea we call Earth.
Yet we tolerate and nurture its insolence.
We ride on a carefree carousel of infidelity,
while we baptize our anemic Tower of Babel.
Blind, deaf and dumb we feed on barbiturates
and smile upon this oppressive behemoth.
Home, sweet home, our catacomb of obituaries.
So we honor the parochial cherub and
the swank servants of the State
while we scour the land like caterpillars,
in search of the sweet honeydew of honesty,
finding only an onion to allow us to cry.

Spring Rain

It's a grey chill that reaches the marrow of your bones,
the dreary dampness that saturates the sky.
Rain pellets so wet even buildings droop and drain.
Thus, is the stamina of the cool spring rains.

Droplets shower down. Shoes slosh through the streets.
Soaked shingles on rooftops shimmer and shine.
Sidewalks stay slick with winter's sprinkled remains.
And slippers stay home to remain free from stains.

Soldiers' cheeks glisten when speckled with sleet.
And crocuses struggle through moist soil to sprout.
Sparrows search for hidden seeds and winter grains,
while the ceaseless pitter patter fails to wane.

Breathe

Breathe in the animated poetry of the morning,
and digest the desserts of yesterday.
Exhale the pallid partnerships of indulgence,
and grow a seed of buoyancy.
Cast out the parasites of meaningless monologues,
and build your nest of clarity.

Unicorns

Like clouded dreams of amber skies,
I amble blindly through a maze of unicorns.
Fantasizing the realities of tortured truths,
making them masters of my contorted memories.
Deformed and grotesque creatures of insanity
rise sanguine from the seas of my satanic obsessions.
Glorious are the barbaric beasts of illusion that
feed endlessly on the power of my hopelessness.

The Spiders

When illusion takes control like a puppet with a heart,
the Master of strings wraps a noose around my courage,
suffocated and bled of my last spiritual nourishment.
The spiders of deceit and hypocrisy spit on my final plea for trust,
and spin a web of fog over my path to freedom.
And the chains of this theater leave me imprisoned in your
dungeon of addiction, as you send your poisoned hatred
for all that is beautiful, and continue to suck forth
my hopes and love, just to feed on their power and tranform
love to hate.

My Home – My Vessel

I shall treasure the small vessel that cradles
the undying virginity of my perfect soul.
Torn, shackled, raped and caressed,
polished by the samsaric seas of famished desires.
Limp from exhaustion it bleeds nectars of hope
into a snake pit of deformed leeches and
collects droplets of cursed curiosities
that evaporate unfed.
Warriors bore through my feminine flask
like convulsed parasites.
Kicked and chipped, I'm restored and repainted,
But remain cracked and scarred.
Vipers and vagabonds, infants and lovers
chisel my vessel in search of shelter.
I cower in its depths.
Beams of solitude grace my container
with tears that dry the staining sweat
of loneliness and fear,
a soliloquy of solitude injected
into my body - insulin of identification.
A corroded cork atop; leaking lacerations below –
My vessel is my treasure.

Glass Houses

I hit the window like a bee seeking warmth,
blind to the glass that separates out and in.
Contusion! Eyes to the sky,
never permitted into your greenhouse.
Solid as ice but as fragile as an icicle,
and ever so transparent.
Yet distorted by darkness inside, and
the laughing crocuses outside.
Snow buries me. Unable to spread
my wings.
The melting flakes soothe
the scars of too many blind flights –
too many inviting glass houses.

My Desert

Gasping, choking, shriveled,
combing the desert for a
droplet of love.
Sands of emptiness, loneliness
pour through my body –
fill my toes, saturate my limbs,
dry my heart.
Spitting up grains of your indifference
lodged in my throat.
Pneumonia cocoons my cells
trapped in a prison of numbness.
The desert's heat turns passions to cinders,
charred remains of all that is gone.
My face, painted in ashen remains,
hides the sand's scars.
Fevered from your scorpion sting,
crawling for an oasis,
dragging, crippled,
in circles toward a mirage of hope
but already blind.
A scream, a song – only deafness.
My head bound by a dune of cacophony.
Moonlight – I freeze.
She smiles on me – frozen, impenetrable.
And the desert snakes hunt
for the warmth of a fire long gone.

Outcast

Acknowledgement of achievement smiles
smugly on the artistry of deceit,
falling prey to the graces of grandiose adequacy.
A flawlessness paralleling the cloning
of common practice and societal norms,
manifested in a live circus that
always rotates clockwise,
in time – in sync – in rhythm, always in step.
An offbeat stray, kicked out like
packed dirt from the circus horse's foot.
Out of the rink, out of the megalopolous
that is modern day society.

The Baby

Recoil, rewind but do not retaliate.
You cannot go back — cannot return.
Erase — rewind — it never happened;
it never was. Water the seed you sliced.
Its gone. You cannot give it life; must
erase — rewind — replant.
A sand trap, quicksand grasps — you gasp.
Never forward. Forward just replays the
Past. A circle. Rewind and erase.
Eradicate and wash, scrub. Frozen, fearful.
Shock, it won't come off; it won't come
Clean. Around and around, no forward movement!
Just clear the footprints or your life will find you
And devour you.

You

I love you because you do bad things, but there is no bad in you.

Do you care? What about? Does it change? Then do you

really care? And why?

You cannot love, but you suffer from love.

You cannot remember, but your memory destroys you.

You cannot feel, but the pain is too much.

You cannot see, but you watch the misery.

You cannot laugh, but you are a clown.

You cannot sleep, but you always dream.

You cannot take, but you always steal.

You cannot give, but are always generous.

You cannot learn, but you always teach.

You keep all inside, but you are always empty.

You always lie, but don't know the truth.

You pack, but you never leave.

You fly, but you never move.

You write, but you have no ink.

You will never win, but you have never lost.

You cannot sing, but I hear your songs.

Your world is dead, but you live in me.

The Devil's Circus - Man

Subscribe to the drama!
A daily dose of sophisticated sophisms.
A prescription of sophomoric songsters.
Sordid delicacies of sour fantasies and
recycled truths manifested in your
passé lingerie. Insulin for the powerless,
nectar for the perverse.
A masochistic orgy of emotional addictions.
Just wallow in the excrement of our self-designed
Reality. Our fantastic three ring circus that is spit
on by the cartoons of the forces above.
Believe in your confirmed miseries and
profess your flawed paradise, barren of compassion,
but fecund with self-pity, and always
claim salvation from our conventional devil.
It's just so easy.

It Died

It's the little things that speak loudly to me.

The way the arms that used to hold me lay flat at your side.

The way the songs, dances and laughs have transformed into the mundane.

Sensual showers become consecutive.

A touch is an apology, not a desire.

Admiration becomes jealously; lust becomes annoyance.

Restraint and guilt corrode your insights.

Confusion

Like the elliptical imperfections of the infinite figure eight,

I am a precise inconsistency. A dedicated unpredictability.

A pristine blemish.

Running to stay ahead of those behind me.

Sprinting to catch those who hold the lead.

I travel not in the middle, but off to the side – to the left of right.

Hailing a taxi but riding a bus, preferring to walk.

Putting my life in no one's hands, my hands in no one's life.

I write to avoid reading and read to avoid thinking.

In the canoe-like pupil of my cat's eyes I am strange, but more
normal than you.

CHAPTER THREE

London
2004 – 2006

The hottest love has the coldest end.

- Socrates

Pain Goes On

The pain continues to punish after the hurt.

You"re weak, like an injured bird, easy prey for vultures.

Lies and fears – the difference is irrelevant.

You want to fly if not for the broken wing.

You stumble, you wobble. Predators smell your frailty.

Your strength is lost. Your pain is heavy. Your fear controlling.

The sky is crowding you; its filled with your tears.

You cannot even see clearly – a helping hand appears as a
warrior's dagger.

Pray

Frantically forcing passivity you resist conversation,

as words beg your attention admitting their own inadequacies.

You brush off sensibilities as your senses grow numb,

as all becomes senseless and remains sensible.

Sensuality seems indifferent and admits defeat.

Turn the page, but the story stays the same.

Switch your suit but you can't swap your style.

You pray to understand prayers -

to understand those who don't understand you.

Silent Scream

I woke to the tender kiss of your breath on my ear.
It whispered comforts that silently caressed my fears.
A warmth of gracefulness calmed my shivering urgency.
Your contagious arms dissolved my solitary grief.
I swam hoping to drown in your nostalgic dreams,
unconscious in the nakedness of your velvet skin.
An orgasm of language screamed in my groin,
words dancing on my tongue, swallowed by my heat.
All rotting in the silence of your magnificent sleep.
Salty tears ran down my choking throat muting
my song of love you cannot hear.

Teach Me

Take me outside so I feel warm inside.

Make me angry so I find peace within.

Tell me lies so I learn to see truth.

Steal my diamonds so I value emptiness.

Beat my bones so I feel the power of numbness.

Starve my body so I learn to feed my mind.

Love me so I remember how to cry.

Go away so that I can be strong again.

Searching

I lose everything I do not need.

I have nothing I need.

My mind perches on a telephone wire.

I search for a seed below,

a nourishment for my thirst,

a thirst for the music of truths.

My Secret

Numbness consumes my fears.

Fatal indifference dries my tears.

I smile smugly, having conquered the desire to feel.

My vision is clear – blind to emotions.

Distractions trampoline off my rubber body.

Your jazzy tunes slide off my icy stare.

My heart pumps solely to keep the rhythm.

A pageantry of lifelessness blooms subtley.

No one knows my secret – no one should.

I can stalk like a panther.

I kill all that is not me,

fascinated by own anomaly,

one so common and so commonly overlooked.

My Untrue Reality

Your warmth is cold and your touch innocuous.
Your innocence cloaked yet your core destructive.
Unsettled like a small pebble in a raging river,
shined to perfection and lost in the tumult of fear.
Rejecting reality, a perpetual emperor in a kingdom
that is trite yet mad, watching only the rainbow ahead.
The albatross and the fairies – I carry strength
for only such a world.
And, as you mount the white steed, I follow you into a hell
colder than blackness.

The Rise that Makes the Fall

My unrelenting loneliness terrorizes my courage.

Its mocking is haunting.

Its power debilitating.

It has no challenger.

I live as its concubine, wallowing in the frozen hell of its silence.

We smile, we wink, we allow no one to learn of our sinister charade.

A sickening prostitution that rots my spirit in secrecy.

A coward made strong by nurturing its own pathetic fear.

Loving to be unloved,

finding pride in the confirmation of its own desperate despair.

An evil made stronger by perpetuating its own immortality,

taking nourishment from the fallacy of fantasies of love.

A tender touch, a sensual smell, a passionate kiss –

a rise that makes the fall more profound,

deepening the lacerations of its grotesque grip.

A slave in your kingdom.

Oh, Loneliness – please,

just a taste of the nectar of love!

No One Really Loves Unless Unloved

Take me on a magic carpet ride.

Drive my sorrow into my gut.

Leave the lies and dreams behind.

No one really loves unless not loved.

My karma keeps me — kills me.

A mystery — my misfortune.

A kiss, a touch, a sympathetic ear.

Drained of my love; left frozen.

To Die With You

My senses released, they swim in a sea of infinite extremes,
devouring the delicate poisons of your fabulous fantasies, and
swallowing the narcotic nectars of your addictive anonymity.
You envelop me in your enigmatic pain choking my reality,
and igniting my hearth of hope.
Helpless I fail to stand under the voodoo of your stare,
quivering on the floor of you delightful dungeon of dreams.
A phantom of the opera operating the puppet strings
that strangle my reality.

Be Strong

Ever the fool you mount the steed from which you tumbled.

Alas, a metallic fixture on the merry-go-round of your pathetic life.

A crowd of critics quick to laugh,

wilted laurels on their corroded crowns.

Get off the ride! Humble to the humiliation,

but never show you paid the fare,

for the farce is too tragic.

Bruises hurt but shall never be bared, and

express your pain through indifference -

an effective way to affect the pained, and indulge the proud.

Scream often, but only into a pillow,

and be a man but only if you are a woman.

Stand tall but feel free to complain about your back.

Watch your back! But never look back.

Forge your weapon, and pray it is never used on you.

My Hour of the Wolf

In the hour of the wolf,

when the sky grows dark,

and the moon comes out to play,

I scurry to hide in the depths of darkness,

like a mole running from light.

My secret is sacred.

Each night I nourish my emptiness in stealth.

As it cries for attention,

I cradle the monstrous child

that I have bred from my own loneliness,

a nightly burden, hungry and needy.

Day breaks, and I bury the satiated pain.

Drained and ragged I proceed through the hours,

my secret secure, awaiting the hour of the wolf.

Step on Me

Step on the back of my hand.

I want to hear my bones crush.

I want to feel your torture.

I want to know your pain,

the pain that brings me such torment.

Blind me so I see not your anger but

feel better your fears.

Starve me so I taste only your madness

and thirst for your freedom.

Chain me so I have reason to break free

from your lies. And

love me so I know you never loved me before.

Listen so you can hear me die inside.

The Battle

Capitalize on the fiery rage that gives you strength
to be irrationally rational,
to use your burning anger to be condescendingly cold.
Nurture your tears to torture your tormentors,
to grow their guilt or quash their assumed conquests.
Maintain haltered passion in your heart,
protecting your spiritual empire and
charge forward dispassionately with an icy fire.
Shhh – display only the piercing pity of a weak woman
in your enviable eyes.
Play the game of the devil, but dance with the angels,
and smile like a child.
Never lose the battle, but don't let on you are engaged in a war.

Love Because We Must

We watch the weary but we weep
not for them but for ourselves.
The emperor's clothes exist but not on you.
So feign fortitude but fear fantasy and
a fool feed, but never be one. And
love because you must. And
live to love but die because you loved.
A tyrant makes you big but the truth small.
We drag the weight of lost love on our
harnessed conscience.
And we quench our thirst for freedom
on the filth of false fidelity.